APEX maths

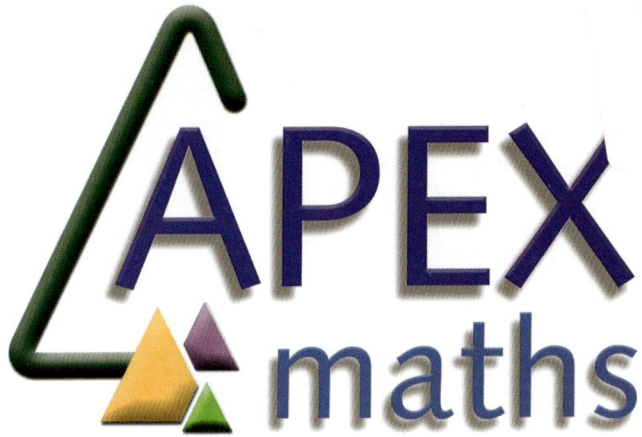

3

Extension *for all* through problem solving

Pupil's Textbook
Year 3 / Primary 4

Ann Montague-Smith

Paul Harrison

CAMBRIDGE UNIVERSITY PRESS

PUBLISHED BY THE PRESS SYNDICATE OF THE UNIVERSITY OF CAMBRIDGE
The Pitt Building, Trumpington Street, Cambridge, United Kingdom

CAMBRIDGE UNIVERSITY PRESS
The Edinburgh Building, Cambridge CB2 2RU, UK
40 West 20th Street, New York, NY 10011-4211, USA
477 Williamstown Road, Port Melbourne, VIC 3207, Australia
Ruiz de Alarcón 13, 28014 Madrid, Spain
Dock House, The Waterfront, Cape Town 8001, South Africa

http://www.cambridge.org

© Cambridge University Press 2003

First published 2003

Printed in Dubai by Oriental Press

Typefaces Frutiger, Swift   *System* QuarkXPress® 4.03

A catalogue record for this book is available from the British Library

ISBN 0 521 75490 9 paperback

Cover design by Karen Thomas

Text illustration by Beccy Blake

Project management by Cambridge Publishing Management Limited

The authors and publishers would like to thank schools and individuals who trialled lessons.

NOTICE TO TEACHERS
It is illegal to reproduce any part of this work in material form
(including photocopying and electronic storage) except under
the following circumstances:
 (i) where you are abiding by a licence granted to your school or institution by the
     Copyright Licensing Agency;
 (ii) where no such licence exists, or where you wish to exceed the terms of a licence, and
     you have gained the written permission of Cambridge University Press;
 (iii) where you are allowed to reproduce without permission under the provisions of
     Chapter 3 of the Copyright, Designs and Patents Act 1988.

> KEY TO TEXT
> Red text: shows things children need for the activity.
> Hint bubbles: give clues to help with the questions.

Contents

1	Our milkman	4
2	Palindromes	6
3	The mysterious dungeon	7
4	The skipping rope	11
5	The fruit bowl	12
6	Close to one hundred	13
7	Which way round?	14
8	Largest and smallest totals	15
9	Total thirty-one	16
10	Telephone numbers	17
11	Make a number	18
12	Shoes, dogs and cats	19
13	Count down to zero	21
14	Four in a row	22
15	A pocketful of money	24
16	Mystery numbers	25
17	Calculator magic	26
18	A street scene	28
19	The blacksmith	29
20	Money box	30
21	Ice cream cones	31
22	Pick up sticks	32
23	Sticky squares	33
24	Squares and triangles	34
25	Fold a shape	35
26	Make that shape	36
27	Jamie's walk	38
28	A weighty problem	40
29	Tennis matches	41
30	Going to the cinema	42

Glossary   **44**

1 Our milkman

Saleem and Debra live in Oak Tree Close. They talk about the milkman who delivers their milk.

"Our milkman uses a crate with room for 16 bottles. But he only puts 12 bottles in the crate. So there are always 4 spaces," says Saleem.

"He always puts the bottles in the crate in a special way. Each row of bottles has an even number. And each column has an even number too," explains Debra.

They don't say how the milkman does this.

The grid is like the milk crate. Use counters on the grid to show where the milk bottles could go.

Can you work out one way of putting the milk bottles in the crate?

Remember, there are always 4 spaces. Try and spread the spaces around the grid.

When you have a solution, write down how you worked it out.

Now find other ways to arrange the bottles.
Can you see any patterns?

2 Palindromes

5005 is a palindrome. You can read it forwards and backwards and it is still the same number.

Sometimes the year date is a palindrome.

1 Start at 100.

How many palindromes can you find between 100 and 500?

2 Start at 500.

How many palindromes can you find between 500 and 1000?

3 Start at 1000.

How many palindromes can you find between 1000 and 10 000?

Think about the methods you are using. Can you see any patterns? Which palindromes come next?

Write each number backwards to check if it is a palindrome. For 123 you would write 321. Now, is that a palindrome?

3 The mysterious dungeon

A wicked dragon has locked 3 knights in a dungeon. They can escape if they know the secret password. Help them to work out the password.

You have 4 number riddles to solve. They are **a**, **b**, **c** and **d** below.

Each riddle makes a 2-digit number.

Work out each digit of the number. Write it down.

1 **a** The tens digit is 9 minus 6.
  The units digit is 4 doubled.

  b The tens digit is 5 more than 4.
  The units digit is 1 less than 4.

  c Multiply 3 by 3.
  That gives you the tens digit.
  The units digit is not 4 but is in the 4 times table.

  d Find the number of months in a year. Now take away the number of days in a week. That gives you the tens digit.
  Multiply 3 by 2. Add 2. Write your answer in the units place.

Write down each number.

Turn to page 10 to work out the password.

3 knights are trapped in a tower.

Help the knights work out the secret password to let them escape.

You have 4 number riddles to solve. They are **a**, **b**, **c** and **d** below.

Each riddle makes a 3-digit number.

Work out each digit of the number. Write it down.

Take care: you don't need some of the clues!

2 a The hundreds digit is half of 2.
    The tens digit is 5 subtract 5.
    The units digit is the tens digit times 4.

  b The units digit is the product of 1 and 1.
    The tens digit is 3 less than 4.
    Add 6 to the tens digit.
    The hundreds digit is the tens digit multiplied by 1.

  c The hundreds digit is the smallest digit. It is more than 1 and less than 3.
    The tens digit is the largest and is double the hundreds digit.
    The units digit is how many socks there are in a pair.

  d Multiply 5 by 10.
    The units digit is the difference between 10 and 7.
    The tens digit is how many halves make one whole.
    The hundreds digit is 10 subtract 7 subtract 2.

Write down each number.

Turn to page 10 to work out the password.

3 knights have escaped from the tower. They are on the roof but the door to the stairs is locked.

Can you help the knights work out the secret password to open the door?

You have 4 number riddles to solve. They are **a**, **b**, **c** and **d** below.

Each riddle makes a 4-digit number.

Work out each digit of the number. Write it down.

Take care: you don't need some of the clues!

3 **a** The thousands digit is the difference between 25 and 17.
The hundreds digit is half the thousands digit.
The tens digit is a quarter of 4.
Subtract 1 from the hundreds digit to find the units digit.

b The thousands digit is half of 10.
The hundreds digit is the thousands digit plus 4.
The tens digit is the product of 6 and zero.
Divide 100 by 20.
The units digit is a third of 9.

c The digit in the units place is a quarter of 16.
The tens digit is half of a dozen.
Double the units digit to find the hundreds digit.
Find the difference between 19 and 37.
Divide 25 by 5 to find the thousands digit.

d Work out half of 46.
The thousands digit is the difference between 32 and 28.
The hundreds digit is a quarter of 24.
Subtract 5 from the hundreds digit to find the tens digit.
The hundreds digit plus the tens digit makes the units digit.

Write down each number.

Turn to page 10 to work out the password.

Use your numbers to help you solve the puzzle.

Take one of your 4 numbers.

Add its digits.

Is the answer more than 1 digit?

Then add those digits.

Keep going until you have just **1 digit**. This is called the **digital root**.

Use the code to find what the digit means. Work out the password.

What is your password?

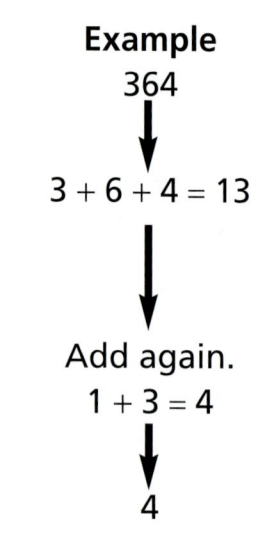

Example
364
↓
3 + 6 + 4 = 13
↓
Add again.
1 + 3 = 4
↓
4

4 is the digital root.

Code:
- look 2
- chimney 4
- up 3
- hidden 5
- climb 1
- key 9
- find 7
- ladder 6
- the 8

4 The skipping rope

Some children wanted to skip together, so they found a really long rope.

But half of it was rotten, so they cut off the rotten half and threw it away.

The rope was still far too long, so they cut off a third more.

They used the rest of the rope for skipping.

1 The rope was 18 metres long to start with.

How long was their skipping rope?

2 What if they started with 24 metres of rope?

How long would their skipping rope be?

3 What if their skipping rope was 10 metres long?

How long was the piece of rope when they first found it?

Do you think that they could skip with a 10 metre long skipping rope?

Explain your thinking.

> Draw a picture of the rope.
> Draw what you know about the rope.
> Think about the fractions that it is being cut into.

5 The fruit bowl

A huge bowl is full of fresh fruit. Use the clues to work out how much fruit is in the bowl.

1 $\frac{1}{2}$ of the fruit are apples.

There are also 2 oranges, 1 pear and 6 bananas.

How many apples are there in the bowl?

How many pieces of fruit are there altogether?

Draw a diagram, if this helps.

2 $\frac{1}{4}$ of the fruit are apples and $\frac{1}{4}$ of the fruit are pears.

There are 6 bananas, 1 orange, 2 plums and 1 peach.

How many apples are there in the bowl?

How many pieces of fruit are there altogether?

3 $\frac{1}{3}$ of the fruit are apples and $\frac{1}{3}$ of the fruit are pears.

There are 5 bananas, 2 oranges and 4 plums, as well as 3 strawberries and a nectarine.

How many apples are there in the bowl?

How many pieces of fruit are there altogether?

Write about how you worked out the answer.

6 Close to one hundred

Use these digits:

1   2   3   4   5   6

and + and =

Find totals that are **as close to 100** as possible.

You must use **all of the digits only once.** You can use the digits in **any order, each time**.

You can use digits to make 2-digit numbers, e.g. 12 + 43.

You can use them as they are, e.g. 5 + 3 + 4 + 2.

Record your calculation each time.

Here are some examples:

13 + 42 + 56 = 111

65 + 43 + 12 = 120

> Which pair of digits makes the largest number?
> Which pair of digits makes the smallest number?
> Which digits can you add to give 0 for the units?

7 Which way round?

You need a set of 1 to 9 digit cards.

1 Choose any 2 digits.

Make a number.

Now swap over the digits to make a new number.

Add your 2 numbers together.

Try again for other numbers.

What do you notice?

Write down a rule.

> Try digits 1, 2, 3, 4 and 5 first.

2 Choose any 3 digits.

Make a number.

Now reverse the digits to make a new number.

Add your 3 numbers together to make a total.

Try again for other numbers.

What do you notice?

Write down a rule.

> Set out your work in an organised way. Can you see any patterns?

8 Largest and smallest totals

You need a set of 0 to 9 digit cards.

1 Choose 4 cards.

Make two 2-digit numbers.

Make an addition sentence like this:

| 3 | 4 | + | 2 | 5 | = |

What is the largest total that you can make with your 4 digit cards?

What is the smallest?

Try different choices of 4 cards.

Write down rules for making the largest and smallest totals.

Where should the largest digit go? And the smallest digit?

2 Choose 6 cards.

Make two 3-digit numbers.

Make an addition sentence like this:

| 3 | 7 | 1 | + | 5 | 2 | 8 | = |

What is the largest total that you can make with your 6 digit cards?

What is the smallest?

Investigate this, trying different choices of 6 cards.

Write down some rules for making the largest and smallest totals.

9 Total thirty-one

You need 24 counters or cubes.

Play this game with a partner.

The aim of the game is to make the total **exactly 31**.

Start with a total of 0.

Take turns to cover a number on the board with a counter.

Add each number you cover to the total.

You share the total, so that each of you adds to it.

If you go over 31 you lose! The winner is the first one to reach 31 exactly.

1	2	3	4	5	6
1	2	3	4	5	6
1	2	3	4	5	6
1	2	3	4	5	6

How can you stop your partner winning? Look carefully at the numbers that are uncovered. Which number should you choose next?

10 Telephone numbers

Jane looked at the buttons on the telephone.

She used the buttons to work out a number for her name.

This is how she did it:

J + A + N + E
5 + 2 + 6 + 3 = 16

Look at which numbers match each letter.

What is your name as a total?

1 How many different names can you find with a number total between 10 and 20?

2 How many different names can you find with a number total between 20 and 30?

3 How many different names can you find with a number total of more than 30?

Do the shortest names always have the smallest totals?

Try different words. Remember that the same number belongs to at least 3 different letters.

11 Make a number

Find different ways of making your total.

You can use addition and subtraction (+ or –).

You can use the same number only **once** in any calculation.

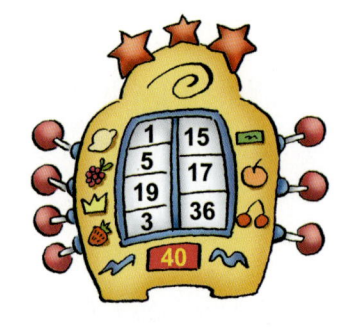

1 These are your numbers: 1   3   5   15   17   19   36

Find different ways of totalling **40**.

2 These are your numbers: 5   17   19   37   39   46   66

Find different ways of totalling **100**.

3 These are your numbers: 10   17   27   45   48   83   85

Find different ways of totalling **120**.

Which way uses the fewest of these numbers to make your total?

Which way uses the most of these numbers to make your total?

Choose pairs of numbers.
What totals can you make?
What is the difference between them?
Now try choosing 3 numbers.

12 Shoes, dogs and cats

1 12 children compared what they were wearing on their feet.

6 of the children had shoes on.

4 of them had socks on.

Only 3 were wearing shoes and socks.

How many children had bare feet?

Write down what you know as number sentences or in pictures.

2 There are 11 dogs.

4 dogs love 'Doggy bites' dog biscuits.

3 dogs enjoy 'Woof 'em down' dog biscuits.

Only 2 of these dogs will eat both 'Doggy bites' and 'Woof 'em down' dog biscuits.

The other dogs will only eat 'Growly' dog biscuits.

How many dogs will only eat 'Growly' dog biscuits?

3 Mrs Jordan has 15 cats. They like different flavours of cat food.

Some of them will only eat fish.

8 of them like rabbit.

4 of the cats prefer chicken.

1 cat eats both rabbit and chicken.

How many cats will only eat fish?

13 Count down to zero

Play this game with a partner.

You need 10 counters each. Choose a different colour each.

31	30	29	28	27	26	25	24
16	17	18	19	20	21	22	23
15	14	13	12	11	10	9	8
0	1	2	3	4	5	6	7

Decide who will go first.

Player 1

Start with the number 31.

Choose a number from 1 to 4.

1   2   3   4

Take away that number from 31.

Leave a counter on the number you reach.

Player 2

Start from the counter number.

Choose a number from 1 to 4.

1   2   3   4

Count back that number.

Leave a counter on the number you reach.

Repeat, taking turns. The winner is the first person to finish on 0.

Can you find a winning strategy?

14 Four in a row

You need counters in 2 different colours.

Play this game with your partner.

Each take 8 counters of one colour.

Take turns to choose **2 numbers** from the list above your grid on page 23.

Multiply these numbers together.

If the answer is on the grid, cover that number with a counter.

The winner is the first to get 4 counters in a row.

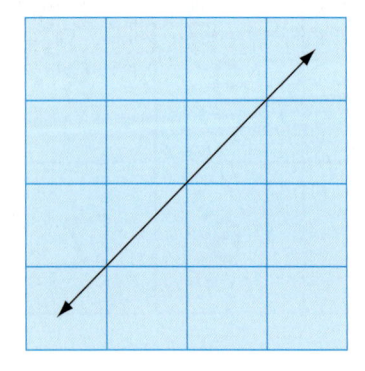

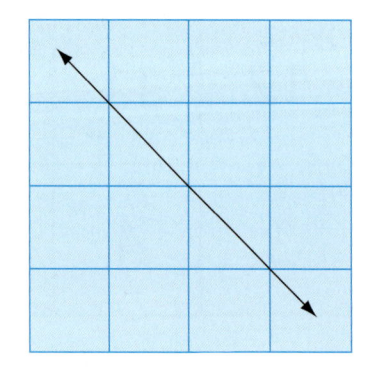

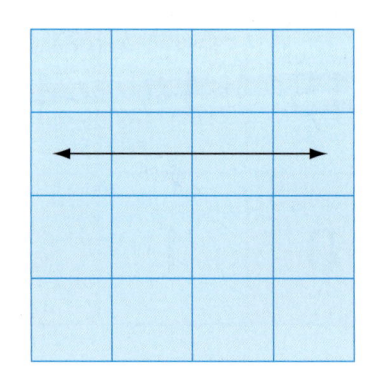

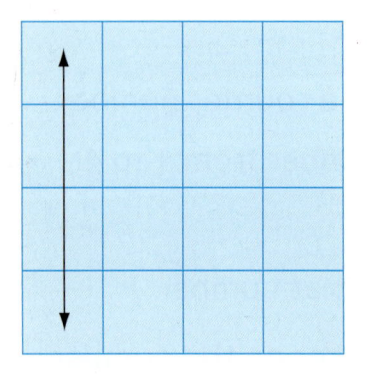

Can you find any strategies for winning this game?

> Use the multiplication facts that you know. Try doubling multiples of 2 to make multiples of 4.

1

| 2 | 3 | 4 | 5 | 10 | 6 | 7 |

6	12	21	10
30	18	30	70
24	60	8	14
20	40	35	15

2

| 15 | 2 | 4 | 10 | 30 | 3 | 5 |

60	150	45	40
8	30	90	300
12	15	30	50
120	10	6	20

3

| 50 | 2 | 95 | 20 | 10 | 3 | 4 |

100	60	20	380
80	40	8	285
950	30	190	200
500	6	12	150

15 A pocketful of money

Daniel, Chloe and Harry have a lot of change in their pockets. They find a vending machine.

1 Daniel buys a chocco Bar. He uses up to 5 coins.

Which coins does he use?

Find different answers.

2 Chloe buys a Fizzo Drink. She uses up to 5 coins.

Which coins does she use?

Find different answers.

3 Harry buys a Fizzo Drink. He uses up to 10 coins.

Which coins does he use?

Find different answers.

16 Mystery numbers

I am thinking of a number. It can be divided exactly by 3. If I divide it by 2, 4 or 5 there is a remainder of 1.

1 Find one number to fit the puzzle that is less than 30.

2 Find one number to fit the puzzle that is greater than 50 and less than 100.

Use a number line or 100 square to help. Which numbers can be divided by 3? Now look for nearby numbers that can be divided by 2, 4 and 5.

17 Calculator magic

You need a calculator, some digit cards and PCM 15 to record your scores.

This is a game for 2 players.

Take turns at being Player 1 and Player 2.

The first player to reach 15 points wins.

Player 1
Take a tens card and a units card.

Make a 2-digit number.

Enter the 2-digit number into the calculator.

Choose 2 more cards and make the **target** 2-digit number.

Player 2
Write a calculation that will change the start number to the target number.

Player 1
Use the calculator to check.

Player 2
Record your score.

Remember! You can only use the calculator after you have written your calculation on the sheet.

You must only press = once each go.

Scoring
Score 1 point for using + or −
Score 2 points for using × or ÷
Score 3 points for using more than one +, −, × or ÷
Score 0 if the number on the calculator at the end is not the target number.

START NUMBER

| Tens | Units |

| Tens pile | Units pile |

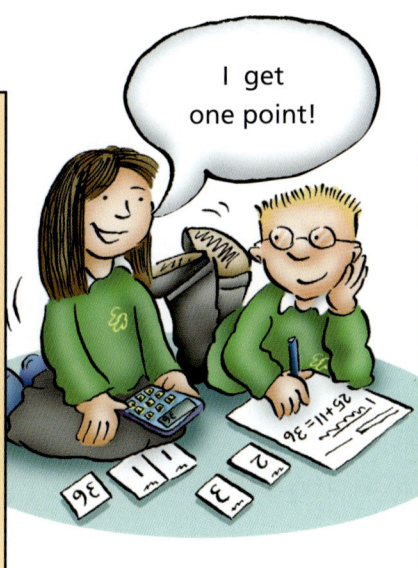

I get one point!

TARGET NUMBER

| Tens | Units |

18 A street scene

James looked out of the window.

He counted the wheels on the vehicles he could see.

Which vehicles do you think he could see?

Write the different possible combinations.

❶ There were 24 wheels.

He could see bicycles and 3-wheeled cars.

❷ There were 36 wheels.

He saw cars with either 3 wheels or 4 wheels.

❸ There were 60 wheels.

He saw cars with either 4 wheels or 6 wheels.

Start with one type of vehicle.
How many of that type of vehicle could there be?
Now try the other vehicle.
What number patterns can you make?

19 The blacksmith

1 Farmer Fred took his horse to the blacksmith.

The horse needed 2 new shoes.

Each shoe needed 4 nails.

He paid 25p for each nail. How much did Fred pay altogether?

2 Farmer Frank's horse needed 2 new shoes. Each shoe needed 4 nails.

He paid like this:
1 penny for the first nail.
2 pence for the second nail.
4 pence for the third nail.
8 pence for the fourth nail.
And so on.

What number pattern can you see?
What would the next number be?

How much did Frank pay altogether?

Who paid more, Fred or Frank?

3 What if each horse needed 3 new shoes?

20 Money box

1 Li empties her money box.

There are 10 coins.

$\frac{1}{2}$ are 50p coins.

She also has a £1 coin, two 2p coins, a 5p coin and a 10p coin.

How much money does she have?

What is half of 10? So how many 50p coins are there in Li's box?

2 Jian empties his money box.

There are 12 coins.

$\frac{1}{4}$ are 10p coins.

Another quarter are 50p coins.

He also has two £1 coins and two £2 coins.

The rest are 5p coins.

How much money does he have?

3 Zeeman has 24 coins in her money box.

$\frac{1}{3}$ are £1 coins.

$\frac{1}{3}$ are 50p coins.

She also has three 20p coins and two 10p coins.

The rest are 5p coins.

How much money does she have?

21 Ice cream cones

On a school visit to the seaside some children decided to buy ice creams.

The stall only sold **double scoop** ice creams, and each had to have 2 **different** flavours.

Ice Cream Flavours
Vanilla
Chocolate
Raspberry
Strawberry
Coffee
Cherry
Orange

Each child chose 2 flavours.

None of the children had the same combination of flavours.

All the possible combinations were chosen.

So how many children bought an ice cream?

Make sure you do not repeat any combinations!

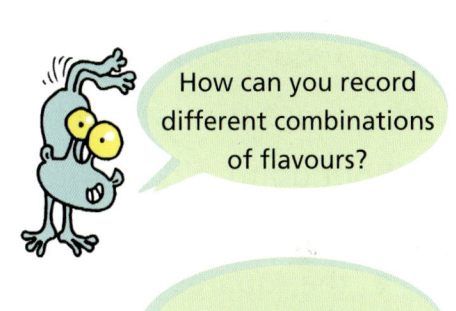

How can you record different combinations of flavours?

Vanilla and chocolate is 1 combination.

22 Pick up sticks

You need sticks or straws.

Make a square like this:

Now make another square next to it, like this:

Make 3 squares, 4 squares, 5 squares, more squares!

Write about the pattern for the number of sticks used each time.

Without using sticks, write how many sticks you will need for:

- all the squares up to 10
- the squares from 11 to 20

Can you work out how many sticks will be needed to make:

- 50 squares?
- 80 squares?
- 100 squares?

23 Sticky squares

You need sticks or straws.

Make a square like this:
Call it: '1'.

1

Problem 1

Add sticks to make an 'L' shape, like this:
Call it '2'.

2

How many sticks does shape '2' use?

Add more sticks to make a larger 'L'.
Call it '3'.
How many sticks does shape '3' use?

Can you find a pattern?
Predict how many sticks you will need for shape '5'.

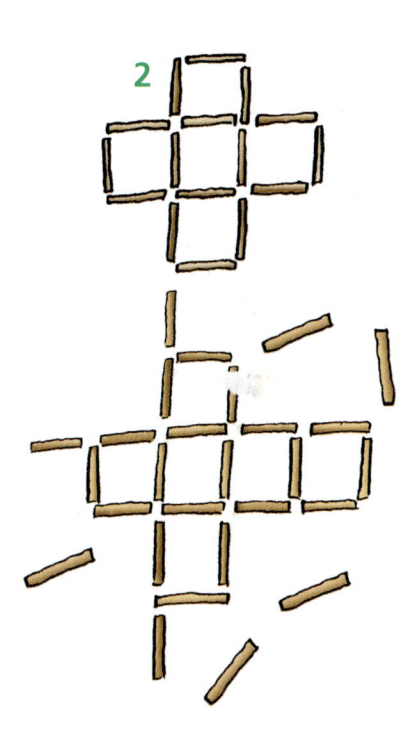

Problem 2

Start with the first square '1'.

Add sticks to make a cross shape, like this:
Call it '2'.

2

Make the cross larger by adding more sticks to each side. Call it '3'.

Now make shape '4' and shape '5'.

How many sticks do you need for each shape?
What number pattern can you see?

Predict how many sticks you will need for shape '10'.

24 Squares and triangles

You need PCM 17 with the shapes cut out.

Remove a right-angled triangle from one of your 'L' shapes by cutting off half a square.

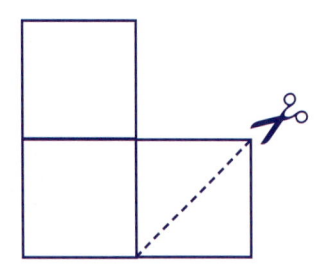

Find different ways of doing this so you get a new shape each time.

Repeat, cutting off 2 right-angled triangles each time.

Draw your shapes on squared paper.

> Check, by turning, that none of your shapes are the same.

Keep your shapes safe. You will need them for another puzzle.

25 Fold a shape

You need some sheets of paper.

Make 1 fold in the paper.

What shape have you made now?

Can you make a shape with 5 sides? 6 sides?

What different shapes can you make?

Glue your finished shapes onto a large piece of paper.

> Try moving the fold to a slightly different place each time.

26 Make that shape

You need these shapes that you made for Lesson 24 Squares and triangles.

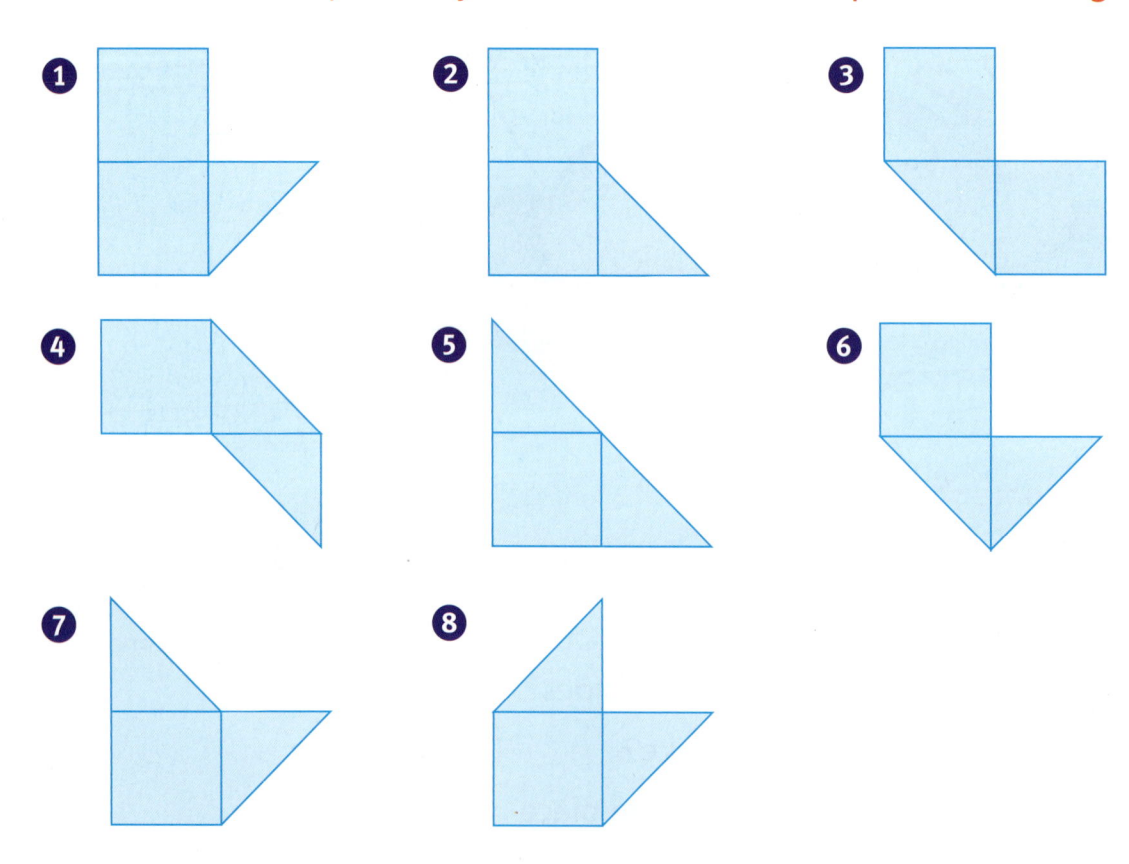

❶ ❷ ❸

❹ ❺ ❻

❼ ❽

Which shapes can you use to cover each shape on page 37?

37

27 Jamie's walk

Jamie's drive is covered in square paving stones.
Look at page 39.

Jamie stands on the cracked stone facing his house.

To get to the waving gnome he:

• walks forward 7 squares

• turns left (makes an anti-clockwise quarter turn)

• walks forward 1 square.

What would be the shortest route from the cracked stone to the garden gate?

Jamie must not crash into garden objects or get his feet wet!

Write down your routes.

What do you notice about the routes that you tried?

Think about how to write down your routes.
Look at the example on this page.
Draw your routes on PCM 19.

39

28 A weighty problem

Every day Mark gives out the maths books to Class 3 at the start of the lesson.

Mark complains to Callum, his best friend, "These books are heavy!"

So Mark and Callum decide to work out how heavy the books are.

Can you help them?

You may only weigh 1 of the maths books in your class.

1. Calculate how much 2 maths books weigh.

   Remember to estimate first!

2. Calculate how much 10 maths books weigh altogether.

   Remember to estimate first!

3. Calculate how much all the maths books in your class weigh if every child has a book.

   Remember to estimate first!

An estimate is a careful guess.
Which units should you use?
Grams or kilograms?
Why?

Extra

Choose a different book, for example an atlas or dictionary, and calculate questions 1, 2 and 3 for this book.

29 Tennis matches

Ramesh, May, Tom and Emily like to play tennis.

They enter the local tennis club tournament.

Each one has to play each of the other three.

All four children lead very busy lives.

Ramesh is not free to play on Tuesday, Wednesday or Saturday.

May can play on Monday, Wednesday and Saturday.

Tom has to stay at home on Monday, Wednesday and Thursday.

Emily can play on Tuesday, Wednesday and Thursday.

On Sundays they all have tennis coaching so none of them are free.

Help each pair to find a day when they can play tennis.

Think about who can play against whom on which day.

Remember – boys and girls can play each other.

When can Ramesh play May?

30 Going to the cinema

Lauren, Sarah and Milly are best friends.

They want to go to the cinema together to see the new Pop Star film.

But they are all so busy!

Can you find a time when they can all go together?

Here is what they are doing.

Sarah's Diary
- Sunday Football 12–4:30 pm
- Monday
- Tuesday
- Wednesday
- Thursday
- Friday
- Saturday Judo 10:30 am – 2 pm

Milly
- Sunday Visit Granny 5–8 pm
- Monday
- Tuesday Swimming 5:30–7:30 pm
- Wednesday
- Thursday Swimming 5:30–7:30 pm
- Friday
- Saturday Swimming 2–3:30 pm

Lauren
- Sunday Dancing class 1–3 pm
- Monday Dancing class 5–8 pm
- Tuesday
- Wednesday Dancing class 5–8 pm
- Thursday
- Friday Dancing class 5–8 pm
- Saturday

They are at school from 9:00 am to 3:30 pm.

They all go to bed at 9:00 pm on a school night.

The film is shown at the cinema at these times:

Monday to Thursday	6:30-8:30 pm
Friday	5:30-7:30 pm 9:00-11:00 pm
Saturday	1:30-3:30 pm 6:30-8:30 pm
Sunday	1:30-3:30 pm 6:30-8:30 pm

Think about the times and if there is school the next day.

How about Wednesday at 7pm?

I can't. I've got dancing.

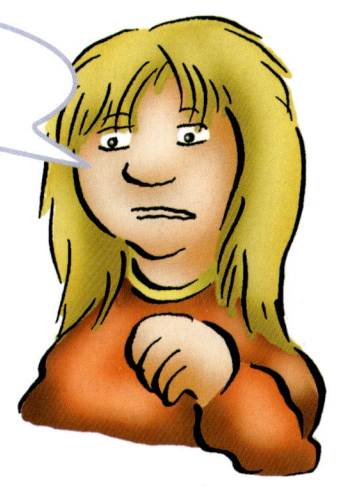

So, when can we go to the cinema?

Glossary

am

am is another way of saying morning. It is the time before midday.

> The opposite is *pm* (afternoon).
>
> **am** comes from the Latin ante meridiem meaning before noon.

> 10 am means
> 10 o'clock in the morning.

calculator

A **calculator** is an electronic instrument that works out the answers to calculations.

clockwise

Clockwise is the way the hands on a clock move.

> The opposite way is anti-clockwise.
>
> An object or person can turn in a clockwise or anti-clockwise direction.

clockwise   anti-clockwise

combination

This is a possible arrangement of objects.

> In this picture the child has chosen chocolate and vanilla ice cream. The **combination** here is chocolate and vanilla.

decrease

This means to get smaller, or to have fewer.

> If Jake gives 2 of his marbles to Lee, Jake's number of marbles **decreases** by 2.

diagonal

A **diagonal** is a line that joins 2 corners of a shape, but is not a side.

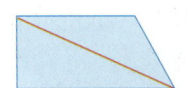

digit

The **digits** are **0 1 2 3 4 5 6 7 8 9**.

> So, in the number 95 the digits are 9 and 5.

digital root

The **digital root** is the final total of digits in a number.

The digital root of **15** is **1 + 5 = 6**.

estimate

An **estimate** is a careful guess.

Looking at something can often help you to estimate its height or weight or how many there are.

even numbers

An **even number** can be divided exactly by 2.

2, 4, 6, 8, 10 … are even numbers.

fraction

A **fraction** is part of a whole shape or number.

A half ($\frac{1}{2}$) is a fraction.

A half of 8 is 4. $\frac{1}{2}$ of 8 is 4.

gram

This is a unit for measuring weight.

1000 **grams** make a kilogram.

half turn

A **half turn** is when an object or person turns 180°. It is like turning half of a circle.

heptagon

A **heptagon** is a flat shape with 7 straight sides.

hexagon

A **hexagon** is a flat shape with 6 straight sides.

increase

This means to get larger, or to have more.

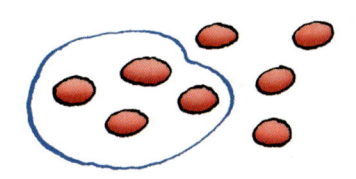

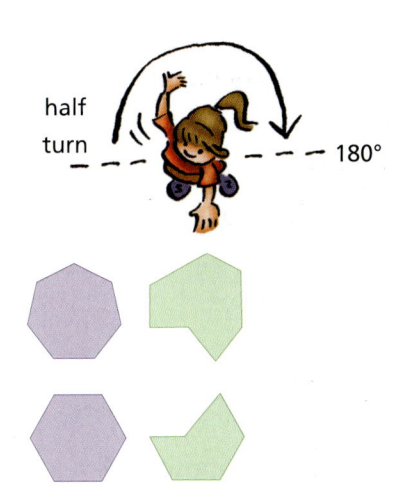

multiple

A **multiple** of a number is an answer in its times-table.

Some multiples of 3 are: 3, 6, 9, 12, 15, 18 …

nonagon

A **nonagon** is a flat shape with 9 straight sides.

numeral

This is a symbol for a number.

The number twenty-five (25) is made up of the **numerals** 2 and 5.

octagon

An **octagon** is a flat shape with 8 straight sides.

palindrome

A **palindrome** is a number that reads the same, forwards or backwards.

These are palindromes: 121   1221

pentagon

A **pentagon** is a flat shape with 5 straight sides.

place value

This tells you how much a digit is worth.

In the number **123**,
1 represents **100**,
2 represents **20** or two tens,
3 represents **3** units or ones.

pm

pm is another way of saying afternoon. It is the time after midday.

The opposite is *am* (morning).

pm comes from the Latin post meridiem meaning after noon.

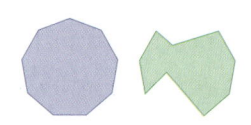

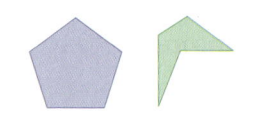

3 pm means
3 o'clock in the afternoon.

product

The **product** is the answer when 2 numbers are multiplied together.

6 × 2 = 12. The product of 6 and 2 is 12.

quadrilateral

A **quadrilateral** is any flat shape with 4 straight sides.

These shapes are all quadrilaterals.

quarter turn

A **quarter turn** is when an object or person turns 90°. It is like turning a quarter of a circle.

reflect

A shape that has been **reflected** makes a mirror image.

remainder

A **remainder** is a number that is left over in a division calculation.

11 ÷ 2 = 5 r1. The **remainder** is 1, or there is 1 left over.

reverse

Reverse means 'opposite way round'.
The *digits* in the number 123 can be reversed to make the number 321.

right-angled triangle

This is a *triangle* that has 1 right angle.

rotate

This means to turn a shape.

The vanes of a windmill **rotate**.

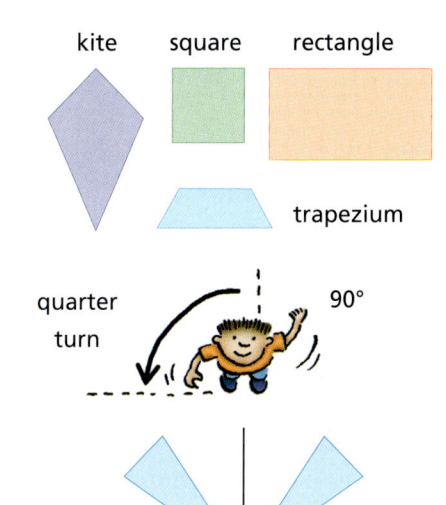

square

A **square** is a flat shape with 4 straight sides the same length and 4 right angles.

timetable

A **timetable** gives information about when something will happen.

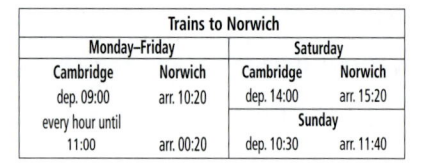

total

A **total** is how many there are altogether. It is the sum found by adding.

$6 + 3 + 5 = 14$. The total is **14**.

triangle

A **triangle** is a flat shape with 3 straight sides.

These are all triangles.

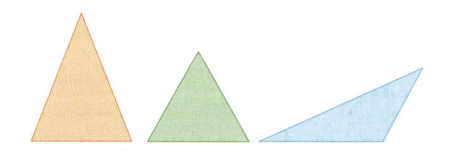